WORSHIP MUSIC HOW TO:
PIANO
BOOK 1

A Practical Guide to Worship Piano

Todd G. Kelly

♪ A Little Slower Music Publishing

Rio Rancho, New Mexico

ISBN: 9798995033608

Library of Congress Control Number: 2026905832

Published by

A Little Slower Music Publishing

First Edition

Cover design and musical engraving by Todd G. Kelly.

TABLE OF CONTENTS

Major and Minor Triad Chords

WORSHIP MUSIC HOW TO: PIANO — BOOK 1

Introduction

You may be just beginning your journey into worship piano, or you may already have some experience and want to grow deeper. Either way, this course is designed for you.

If you're brand new, this book will feel fast-paced. But if you're far enough along to know the names of the keys, understand sharps and flats, have a basic sense of rhythm, and are willing to sing, this book will serve you well.

My approach is simple and practical. We'll use theory—but only enough to explain why things work. Not heavy academic theory. Functional theory that you can immediately use at the keyboard.

At its core, music theory provides reliable choices resulting from the interplay between math, rules, and creativity. We use math as a framework for the rules. The math explains structure—how music is built—but the math itself isn't the music. The real theory is in how those rules are applied—how we choose what to play, when to play it, and sometimes when to bend or even break the rules.

That's where creativity lives. That's where music becomes expressive instead of mechanical.

The possibilities are endless. The goal of this book isn't to cover everything, but to give you a clear starting point—just a handful of useful choices that will help you play worship music with understanding, confidence, and intention.

Some early chapters may feel basic. Stay with them anyway. They are an important foundation for everything that follows—part of a larger pathway for learning worship piano, forming a complete progression—from understanding how music works—to playing confidently from charts—to creating your own usable arrangements.

Think of this book less as something you study and more as something you absorb through practice. Train your hands. Train your ears. Move steadily, but don't rush. What you build here becomes the groundwork for everything that follows.

With that in mind, welcome to:

WORSHIP MUSIC HOW TO: PIANO — BOOK 1.

Chapter 1

The Parts of Music

Melody, Harmony, Rhythm

There are many parts of music, some small and some large. Three main parts, however, are especially important to understand: melody, harmony, and rhythm. Let's explore.

Melody is the tune—the part you sing, hum, or whistle. Melody is the main point or theme of the music and often the most easily identifiable part. I like to think of melody as the signature tune. Our signature identifies us as unique individuals. Melodies identify each song as unique. Good melodies are easy to remember; they stick with you.

One more important thing about melody: melodies come from scales. We'll learn more about scales in Chapters 3, 4, 5, and 9.

Harmony happens when two or more notes sound together. Generally speaking, harmony notes sound good together, and they also support the melody. Harmony adds background, depth, texture, and mood to the overall sound. The simplest kind of harmony has two notes, called intervals. Three or more notes sounding together form chords. We'll learn more about chords in Chapters 7 and 8.

Rhythm is the arrangement of sounds and silences into patterns in relation to a steady beat. The sounds we call notes, and the silences we call rests. A beat is a steady, equal pulse of time. Rhythm patterns drive the music forward. There is much more to know about rhythm, but for now, at least remember this: rhythm is patterns of beats.

Pick a worship song you already know by heart.

1) Melody (the tune)

☐ Hum the melody

☐ Now sing it using "la-la-la" (no words)

☐ Now sing the words

Question: Can you hear the tune clearly, by itself (without harmony)?

2) Harmony (the support)

Now play any single chord you know (C is fine—or a chord from your chosen song) and sing a melody over it. Use your imagination. Sing the notes of the chord one at a time in broken-chord fashion. Sing the notes in different orders—experiment. Play all the notes together at the same time in block-chord fashion.

☐ How do the chord notes sound when played one at a time?

☐ How do they sound when played all together?

☐ Do you notice how melodies can come from the chord tones?

3) Rhythm (the pattern)

Listen for the pulse, the underlying beat that drives the music forward.

☐ Can you snap your fingers, clap your hands, or stomp your feet to the beat?

☐ Can you count out loud? 1–2–3–4 (or 1–2–3)

☐ Can you keep the count going while you hum the melody?

Goal check

☐ I can point to melody, harmony, and rhythm in a real song

☐ I can keep a steady beat while singing or humming

To wrap up this chapter, consider: In worship music, melodies are often simple and singable, harmonies support the song without overpowering it, and rhythms are steady so the congregation can stay together.

Chapter 2

How Harmony Moves

Let's start with an organizing system called the Circle of 5ths. The Circle of 5ths is usually not introduced this early in music theory, but in this course we are moving fast. So what is the Circle of 5ths, and why is it important?

The Circle of 5ths is simple—and profound. Simple because it's easy to learn. Profound because almost everything in music relates to it.

Most common chord movement in the music of Western culture? 5 to 1. Dominant to Tonic. This will be explained a little later, but if you can count to five, you can understand this.

The Circle of 5ths will be covered more thoroughly in Book 2. For now, just remember this: the Circle of 5ths is the key to understanding scales, intervals, chords, and key signatures. At this stage, we'll use it simply as an order for learning scales.

To help with that, here is a sentence I want you to memorize:

Father Charles Goes Down And Ends Battle

This sentence doesn't make perfect grammatical sense, but it does tell a story, and it's easy to remember. The purpose of this sentence is to recall the order of the first letters of each word:

F – C – G – D – A – E – B

Going backwards through the sentence gives you this story:

Battle Ends And Down Goes Charles Father

And the reverse order:

B – E – A – D – G – C – F

Practice saying and playing this order forwards and backwards. Both directions show up constantly in real music.

If you organize your basic practice around the Circle of 5ths, you'll begin to recognize the most common and effective chord movements.

Over time, this foundation will help you unlock how harmony moves and how music works.

See Example 1 on Page 64: Circle of Fifths — Primary Pathway

 STUDENT PRACTICE BOX: THE PATHWAY DIFFERENT WAYS

Once you know the order, it's time to loosen it up.

These exercises are about keyboard awareness, not speed.

Linear Order

Play the notes straight up the pathway, then straight back down.

Forward:

F – C – G – D – A – E – B. (Father Charles Goes Down And Ends Battle).

Backward:

B – E – A – D – G – C – F. (Battle Ends And Down Goes Charles Father).

☐ Play slowly

☐ Use any finger

☐ Listen for how familiar this already sounds

This is the most basic form. Let's try a couple others:

Zigzag Order

Now play the same notes, but alternate direction each time.

Starting on F:

Up to C

Down to G

Up to D

Down to A

Up to E

Down to B

You're still following the same order—you're just changing direction.

☐ Stay relaxed

☐ Don't rush

☐ Let your hand move naturally

Right-Hand Fingering

Use a simple 1–5–1–5 pattern as you step up and down.

Thumb (1) on the lower note

Pinky (5) on the upper note

For Left Hand it's the opposite: Pinky (5) on the lower note

Thumb (1) on the upper note

As the line zigzags, your hand opens and closes naturally while staying relaxed. This fingering reinforces balance, spacing, and keyboard geography without locking you into one position. This order keeps the entire movement within an octave.

Improvised Order

Now for the fun part.

Keep the note order intact, but find each note anywhere you want on the keyboard.

Low, high, middle—it's up to you

Change octaves freely

Change directions at will

Explore the full keyboard

There's no right or wrong here.

☐ Keep the order

☐ Explore the geography

☐ Trust your hands

This turns the pathway into something you own, not something you memorize.

See Example 2 on page 65: Circle of 5ths — Same Order — Different Pathway.

Notice how these orders are based exactly on the Circle of 5ths. The distance from one key to the next going clockwise around the circle is 5 scale degrees—a 5th. The distance between two keys is called an interval. Practicing these interval orders is an imaginative way that helps instill the Circle of 5ths into your mind and fingers.

Chapter 3

Scales Are the Foundation — The Building Blocks

Scales are the foundation of all music. As we've already learned, melodies come from scales—and so do intervals and chords. A scale is a specific pattern of half-steps and whole-steps that creates a framework for music.

Half-Steps and Whole-Steps

Half-steps and whole-steps are the building blocks of scales.

Half-Steps

A half-step is the shortest distance between two keys on the piano. It's one key to the very next—you never skip a key. If you start on a white key, the black key immediately to the right or left is a half-step.

Example:

Starting on D, the half-step up is D♯ (D sharp), and the half-step down is D♭ (D flat).

A sharp (♯) raises a note by a half-step, and a flat (♭) lowers a note by a half-step.

A quick memory trick: Sharp nails go up—flat tires go down.

Most half-steps occur between a white key and a black key. However, there are two white-key half-steps: B–C and E–F.

Music structure: The chromatic scale uses only half-steps.

Music example: The classic "circus theme" sound is based on the chromatic scale.

Whole-Steps

A whole-step is a half-step plus a half-step. With whole-steps, you always skip one key in between.

Examples:

C–D is a whole-step because you skip the black key between them.

E–F♯ is a whole-step because you skip a white key between them.

Whole-steps can occur between:

- two white keys
- two black keys
- a white key and a black key (either direction)

Music structure: Whole-tone scales use only whole-steps.

Music example: The introduction to Stevie Wonder's "You Are the Sunshine of My Life" features a whole-tone sound.

■■■ STUDENT PRACTICE BOX: HALF STEPS ■■■

What is a half step?

A half step is the shortest distance between two keys on the keyboard—one key to the very next. Don't skip a key.

1. At the piano, find and play each half-step pair.

Going up the keyboard:

C–C♯   C♯–D   D–D♯   D♯–E

E–F   F–F♯   F♯–G   G–G♯

G♯–A   A–A♯   A♯–B   B–C

Going down the keyboard:

C–B   B–B♭   B♭–A   A–A♭

A♭–G   G–G♭   G♭–F   F–E

E–E♭   E♭–D   D–D♭   D♭–C

☐ Play slowly

☐ Say or sing the note names, or just sing "la-la-la"

☐ Use one finger if needed

2. Think

A half step is the distance between:

☐ two white keys

☐ two black keys

☐ the closest two keys on the keyboard

Circle all the half steps below:

C–C♯   E–F   B–C   F–F♯   D–E

3. Goal check

☐ I can find half steps starting on any key

☐ I can hear the sound of a half step going up and down

 STUDENT PRACTICE BOX: WHOLE STEPS

What is a whole step?

A whole step is the distance of two half-steps on the keyboard—a half-step plus a half-step. You always skip one key in between.

1.   At the piano, find and play each whole-step pair.

2.   Going up the keyboard:

C–D   C♯–D♯   D–E   D♯–F

E–F♯   F–G   F♯–G♯   G–A

G♯–A♯   A–B   A♯–C   B–C♯

Going down the keyboard:

C–B♭   B–A   B♭–A♭   A–G

A♭–G♭   G–F   G♭–E   F–E♭

E–D   E♭–D♭   D–C   D♭–B

☐ Play slowly

☐ Say or sing the note names, or just sing "la-la-la"

☐ Use one finger if needed

2. Think

A whole step equals:

☐ one half-step

☐ two half-steps

☐ three half-steps

Circle the whole steps below:

C–D   E–F   B–C   F–G   A–B   A#–B   G♭–A♭   D♭–E♭   C#–D

3. Goal check

☐ I can find whole steps starting on any key

☐ I can hear the difference between half steps and whole steps

C–D   E–F   B–C   F–G   A–B   A#–B   G♭–A♭   D♭–E♭   C#–D

Chapter 4

The Major Pentascale

Now we're ready for one of the most important scales in this book: the Major Pentascale. A major pentascale is a bright-sounding, five-note scale that forms the foundation of much worship music. It's simple, musical, and easy to hear. If you can count to five, you can understand this scale.

Before building it, let's review two important terms:

Tonic (1): the home tone

Tonic is where you usually begin and end

Dominant (5): the 5th note of the scale that suggests a return home

Dominant is often played just before going back to Tonic

The tonic is where music feels settled and at rest. The dominant creates motion and tension and wants to return to the tonic.

Building the Major Pentascale

To build a major pentascale, start on the tonic (1) and follow this pattern of steps:

Tonic – Whole – Whole – Half – Whole

Written as a formula:

T – W – W – H – W

This pattern takes you from 1 to 5—from the tonic to the dominant. As you move through the pentascale, notice how the 1 firmly establishes the sense of "home," and how the 5 wants to return home.

 STUDENT PRACTICE BOX: THE MAJOR PENTASCALE 

What is a major pentascale?

A major pentascale is a five-note scale built from 1 to 5 using the pattern:

T – W – W – H – W

1. Build and play

At the piano, start on the tonic (1) and build a major pentascale using the step pattern above.

Example: C Major Pentascale

C – D – E – F – G

1   2   3   4   5

☐ Start on the tonic

☐ Follow the step pattern carefully

☐ Play slowly and evenly

☐ At first, use only one finger, and play the scale up and down until you see the pathway and can remember it

☐ Next, use all your five fingers, called pentascale position, or in this case simply, C position

2. Say and listen

Say the scale degrees out loud as you play: 1–2–3–4–5

Play it and say it backwards too

Then say, or better yet, sing the note names

Listen for the bright, settled sound

☐ I can hear where the scale feels "at home" (1)

☐ I can hear how 5 wants to return to 1

For a notated example, see Example 3 on page 66: Major Pentascale Formula

3. Try it again

Build a major pentascale starting on a different key:

Starting note (tonic): _______________

Notes: _________________________________

Dominant note: _______________

4. Goal check

□ I can build a major pentascale starting on any key

□ I understand how whole-steps and half-steps create the pattern

□ I can hear tonic (1) and dominant (5)

Putting It All Together: The Major Pentascale Pathway

Remember the story about Father Charles?

Father Charles Goes Down And Ends Battle

F – C – G – D – A – E – B

Use this sequence to order your practice of major pentascales. It will help you establish a strong sense of the movement of harmony and provide a solid foundation going forward. I strongly want you to notice that in using this order, the dominant of each scale becomes the tonic of the next. That's an extremely important idea, as it establishes the relationship between chord movement, physical movement, and knowledge of how music works!

 STUDENT PRACTICE BOX: MAJOR PENTASCALE PATHWAY ▨▨▨

1. Find the pathway

Using the Father Charles sentence, build and play the Major Pentascales starting on:

F → C → G → D → A → E → B

☐ Use the T − W − W − H − W pattern

☐ Think 1−2−3−4−5 as you play

2. Start simple

Begin by using one finger (pointer finger) to find the correct keys.

Repeat each pentascale several times until you remember the pathway.

3. Add correct fingering

Once the notes feel comfortable:

Right Hand (RH): 1–2–3–4–5

Left Hand (LH): 5–4–3–2–1

Practice:

☐ RH alone

☐ LH alone

☐ Both hands together (BH)

4. Numbers matter

As you play, always associate each note with its scale degree:

1 – 2 – 3 – 4 – 5

This builds strong connections between sound, number, and keyboard geography.

□ I can name the notes

□ I can say the numbers

□ I can connect both

One of the best ways to learn Major Pentascales is to sing while you play. You don't need to sing well—you just need to try. Your ability to sing the correct notes, called pitch matching, will improve with consistent practice. Don't give up.

The goal isn't to make you a singer. The goal is to connect what you hear inside—to your fingers—to the keyboard—and back to your ears. This circular connection—or circuit—is one of the most powerful ways of learning.

What should you sing?

- Simple syllables: la–la–la, me–me–me, so–so–so, etc.

- Note names

- Numbers

Example: F Major Pentascale

Sing the note names:

F – G – A – B♭ – C

Sing forward and backward:

F – G – A – B♭ – C – B♭ – A – G – F

Sing the numbers:

1 – 2 – 3 – 4 – 5 – 4 – 3 – 2 – 1

Sing the information.

Make up your own lyrics.

The more ways you experience the scale—playing, saying, singing—the faster it becomes natural.

(This book only covers scales that begin on white keys. Scales that begin on black keys will be handled in Book 2.)

Chapter 5

A Scale Becomes a Melody

Everyone knows the tune to "Mary Had a Little Lamb." It's a simple song that fits perfectly within the Major Pentascale.

Because the melody is already familiar, we don't need to focus on written rhythms. Instead, we'll use numbers to show you what to play. These numbers represent scale degrees, not finger numbers.

Starting on the tonic note F, play the tune by following the numbers of the scale. Let the melody you can already hear in your head guide you.

Ma-ry had a   lit-tle lamb | lit-tle lamb | lit-tle lamb

3   2   1   2   3 3   3 | 2   2   2 | 3   5   5

Ma-ry had a   lit-tle lamb | whose fleece | was white as snow

3   2   1   2   3 3   3 | 3   2 | 2   3   2 1

Practice this tune often until it flows smoothly and sounds singing and musical, not mechanical.

You're not trying to sound "correct."

You're trying to sound singing and musical.

1) Ten-Times Rule

Play the melody ten times:

- Slowly and accurately

- Smoothly and connected

- Singing and expressively (like you're telling a story, only with sound)

2) No-Stopping Rule (Short Version)

Play the first phrase without stopping—even if you mess up.

☐ Keep going

☐ Circle the trouble spot

☐ Fix it after. Think of mistakes as gathering information leading to understanding.

Now that you can play Mary Had a Little Lamb, it's time to transpose. To transpose simply means to change position—or change keys.

In chapter 4 you learned how to build the Major Pentascale starting on:

F – C – G – D – A – E – B

With practice, you should be able to play Mary Had a Little Lamb in any of these keys, using the same number pattern every time.

Quick Transpose Check

Pick one or more new keys from the Father Charles pathway:

F – C – G – D – A – E – B

Starting key: _______________

☐ Play the pentascale first

☐ Then play the melody by numbers

Goal check

☐ My melody flows without sounding mechanical

☐ I can transpose it to at least one new key

Chapter 6

The Bass Line

Now that you can play Mary Had a Little Lamb in several different keys, let's add a simple harmony part called a bass line.

The bass line is a single note played in the left hand (LH). For Mary Had a Little Lamb, our bass line will consist of the 1st, 4th, and 5th notes of the scale.

To combine the melody and bass line, the LH numbers are aligned directly beneath the RH numbers. Remember: these are scale degrees, not finger numbers.

ADDING A BASS LINE TO YOUR MELODY

Mary Had a Little Lamb (with Left-Hand Bass Line)

```
      Ma-ry had  a   lit-tle  lamb | lit-tle  lamb | lit-tle  lamb

RH: 3   2  1     2   3   3   3   | 2  2    2    | 3  5    5

LH: 1            1             | 5             | 1
```

Ma-ry had a   lit-tle lamb | whose fleece | was white as snow

RH: 3   2   1   2   3   3   3 | 3   2 | 2   3   2   1

LH: 1   1 | 4 | 5   1

Play the LH notes at the same time as the RH notes they align with. Notice how the LH stays in one position, just like the RH.

Try this project in all the keys you know so far:

F – C – G – D – A – E – B

Chapter 7

Major and Minor Triad Chords

A triad is a three-note chord. The two types we're most interested in right now are the Major Triad and the Minor Triad.

If you play the 1st, 3rd, and 5th notes of the Major Pentascale, you've built a Major Triad.

You can play the notes:

- together (block chords), or

- separately (broken chords)

Using what you already know, you can now find and play:

F, C, G, D, A, E, and B Major Triads

 MAJOR INTO MINOR

The word major describes a sound that is bright and happy. Minor sounds are darker, more sad. The difference is small, but the emotional impact is dramatic.

To change a Major Triad into a minor triad, simply lower the 3rd by a half-step.

To label minor chords, add a lowercase m:

F → Fm   C → Cm   G → Gm   etc.

Now try playing these chords, changing from Major to minor and back again to experience the shift in emotion.

Just for Fun: Minor Mary

Try this version of Mary Had a Little Lamb by lowering the 3rd to change the mood—big time:

Ma-ry had a   lit - tle lamb | lit-tle lamb | who was lost

m3 2 1   2   m3 m3 m3 | 2 2   2 | m3 5   5

Ma-ry went to find her lamb | and bring it | right back home

m3 2 1   2 m3   m3   m3 | m3 2   2 | 3   2   1

The change to minor is reflected in the different lyrics. This is an example of sound emotion supporting the lyrics—a sad story gets a sad sound.

But there's a happy ending when Mary went to find her lamb—reflected in the change from m3 to 3 toward the end. It brightens the mood to support the lyrics, "right back home." Can you add the bass line to this version of Minor Mary?

Chapter 8

Melody Is Tops

You're now ready to move to the next level of chords: Melody Position Inversions. You already know that a triad is built from the 1st, 3rd, and 5th notes of the scale. But those notes don't always have to be played in the order 1–3–5.

For example, you can also play them as:

- 3–5–1

- 5–1–3

When the order of the notes changes like this, the chord is said to be inverted. To invert something simply means to turn it upside down.

Think of it this way:

Put the 5 on top

Then put the 1 on top

Then put the 3 on top

THE KEY IDEA: MELODY POSITION

In melody position chords, the top note matters most. The top note is usually the melody note, and it is the melody note that names the chord position.

Each version is a different melody position of the same chord.

For example:

C major — position of 5, because the 5 is on top — 1 - 3 - 5

C major — position of 1, because the 1 is on top — 3 - 5 - 1

C major — position of 3, because the 3 is on top — 5 - 1 - 3

See Example 4 on page 67: Melody Position Triad Inversions.

Learning the Melody Positions

You will need to become comfortable recognizing and playing all three melody-position triads.

For the purposes of this course, focus on right hand only (RH) and on these chords:

- C major

- F major

- G major

- A minor

The fastest and most permanent way to learn these chords is to say the name of each chord out loud as you play it. Play them going forwards and backwards.

For example, say:

- F major, position of 5

- F major, position of 1

- F major, position of 3

Saying the names while playing is not optional—it's how you teach yourself.

SAY IT AS YOU PLAY IT

☐ Name the chord

☐ Name the melody position

☐ Play the chord

This connects sound, shape, and language in your brain.

Position of 5:   1–3–5

Position of 1:   1–2–5

Position of 3:   1–3–5

Use these fingerings consistently. Good fingering builds speed, accuracy, and confidence.

When playing real music, you will find it handy to sometimes use 1–2–4 fingerings when transitioning from one chord to the next.

What you should be able to do by the end of this chapter

☐ Identify the melody note in a triad

☐ Play all three melody positions of a chord

☐ Name each chord and position out loud

☐ Feel how the change in melody note changes the sound

☐ Sing and identify where the 1, 3, and 5 are as they move in each position

Chapter 9

Charts — Just the Gist

We're ready to jump into charts. In many ways, we've been heading here since Chapter 1. Charts are the most common way music is represented on the page in worship settings, and learning how to read them comfortably will open up a lot of doors.

What a Chart Is (and Isn't)

Charts are bare-bones frameworks for songs. They're almost the opposite of traditional notated music like you'd find in a hymnal or classical score.

A chord chart—sometimes called a lyric chart—gives you just three main pieces of information:

- Song form (verse, chorus, etc.)

- Lyrics

- Chord symbols

That's it.

There are:

- No written notes

- No rhythms

- No dynamics

- No specific chord positions

All of the musical detail comes from the recording, not the page.

Where the Music Comes From

Charts are built on the assumption that you will listen.

Worship musicians spend a lot of time learning songs directly from recordings—essentially playing by ear to discover:

- Melodies

- Riffs and fills

- Bass movement

- Rhythmic feel

- Chord positions

The chart doesn't tell you how or what to play. It simply tells you what's happening and where you are in the song.

This book is not about copying a recording note-for-note. It's about learning how to build your own usable parts from a chart.

In our first venture into charts, we'll be working toward clear goals:

- Create and play a solo piano arrangement that includes:

    ◦ Melody

    ◦ Harmony

    ◦ Bass line

- Create and play an accompaniment part suitable for a worship team

How to Read the Chart

First, don't let the chart intimidate you. A chart is just a framework designed to give you an overview of the music.

■■■ STUDENT PRACTICE BOX: 3 STEPS TO CHART CONFIDENCE ■■■

1) Point and speak

Look at the chart and point as you speak:

☐ Sing the lyrics out loud

☐ Say the chord names only where they appear

2) One chord at a time

With your right hand only:

☐ Play each chord once when you reach it

☐ Hold it (don't worry about rhythm yet)

Do this as many times as you need to get comfortable. Play it at least ten times (the Ten-Times Rule), and repeat several times each day.

3) Add the voice

Now sing or hum the line and change chords only where the chart shows.

Goal check

☐ I can follow the chart without freezing

☐ I can change chords in the right spots while singing

First Chart — Amazing Grace

Amazing Grace is a great song to start with because almost everyone already knows the melody. That familiarity makes it much easier to focus on the chords and their relationship to the melody.

This chart is presented in its simplest form: lyrics only, with chord symbols (bold capital letters) placed directly above the word—or syllable—where the chord changes.

Below is the chart exactly as we'll be working with it.

Amazing Grace—John Newton—Public Domain

<pre>
  C   F   C
Amazing Grace, how sweet the sound

      C   G
That saved a wretch like me

  C   F   C
I once was lost, but now I am found

    Am   G6   C
Was blind, but now I see
</pre>

Finding Melody-Position Chords

The first thing we'll do is find the melody position chords. You should be at your keyboard.

The opening chord is C major. Notice that the chord symbol C is placed above the "m" in A-ma-zing. That tells us exactly where the chord comes in—and that's where we determine the melody position.

Try singing the opening lyric:

A-ma-zi-ng Grace

Notice that the word Amazing is divided into four sung syllables, even though it has three spoken syllables. The melody uses four notes, so for musical purposes, we sing Amazing as four syllables.

Example

   C

A - ma - zi - ng   Grace

g c   e c   e

The lowercase letters below the words represent the melody notes you sing. Notice that the melody note under the "m" in Amazing is c. In the chart, the chord symbol **C** is placed above that same syllable.

So we ask ourselves:

What number is **C** in a **C** chord?

The answer is 1.

Now we know a beautiful sounding position for the opening chord: **C1**—a **C** chord with the 1 on top.

Continuing On

     F   **C**

how sweet the sound

d   c   a   g

This phrase is simpler because each word has one syllable and one melody note.

Notice:

- The **F** chord is over sweet

- The melody note under 'sweet' is c

Since c is the 5 of the **F** chord, the melody position is **F5**.

Also, g being under 'sound' and the chord being **C**, what position will the **C** chord be in?

By now you should be starting to get the idea, so I'll give you one more line—then you'll work the rest on your own.

C1   **G1**

That saved a - a   wretch like me

g   c   e - c e   d   g

The unique thing about this phrase is the splitting of 'a' into two sung syllables to accommodate the two melody notes e and c.

A Note About Lyrics and Melody

Lyrics and melody don't always line up one-to-one.

Words may have a certain number of spoken syllables, but the melody may stretch those words across more notes. When this happens, we don't change the melody—we adjust the way we sing the word to fit it.

This is very common in songs, and it's something you'll want to be aware of.

Application

Play the chords in their correct melody position using your right hand. Keep your chords in the range around middle C.

As you play, try singing along. Only play the chords when you sing the lyrics they harmonize. You can simply hold the chord for now—no rhythmic complexity is needed.

You are reinforcing the connection between melody, harmony, and timing.

You'll notice the **G6** chord symbol in the last line. The scale numbers are 1-3-6, the letters are g-b-e. In this case, the 6 is played instead of the 5 since the melody note is just outside of the triad. This sort of thing will be covered in greater detail in chapter 10.

Now add a simple bass line.

Place your left hand in a C major pentascale position two octaves below middle C.

    c – d – e – f – g

LH: 5 4 3   2   1

Play the note of the chord in the bass at the same moment the chord changes in your right hand.

When playing 'a' under the **Am** chord, simply move your thumb (1) to 'a' to keep it close to 'g' coming up next.

Keep it simple.

The goal is coordination, not complexity.

You're now almost ready to create a solo piano arrangement—complete with melody, chords, and bass line. But first, we need to expand your melodic range.

Chapter 10

Expanding Your Melodic Range

Up to now, we've worked mostly with the major pentascale. That was intentional.

The pentascale gives you strong control over chords, harmony, and basic melody. In fact, a surprising amount of real music lives comfortably within those five notes.

But melodies do reach higher—or lower. When that happens, we expand beyond the pentascale into the complete major scale.

Think of this not as a new system, but as an expansion of the one you already know. As we move forward, you'll see two ideas working side by side:

- Pentascale thinking for chords

- Complete scale thinking for melody

Same system. Different focus.

From Five Notes to Eight

A pentascale contains five notes: 1-2-3-4-5

A complete major scale has eight notes: 1-2-3-4-5-6-7-1

The final 1 is simply the tonic at a higher pitch. The distance from the first 1 to the next is called an octave. (An octopus has eight arms. An octave has eight notes.)

When you reach the octave, you've traveled through the full melodic range of the scale and arrived back home at a higher pitch.

Letters and Numbers Working Together

A complete major scale uses seven different letter names, but the first letter appears twice—at the beginning and the octave.

Example: A Major

1   2   3   4   5   6   7   1

A – B – C♯ – D – E – F♯ – G♯ – A

Because letters and numbers line up, the home tone (tonic) is always 1, no matter where it appears on the keyboard. Once you get this idea, everything else starts to feel much more organized.

The numbers always tell you function. The letters tell you pitch.

No matter where you begin on the keyboard, 1 is always home.

Once this connection between letters and numbers becomes natural, the keyboard feels organized instead of overwhelming.

The Major Scale Formula

You already know the major pentascale formula:

T – W – W – H – W

The complete major scale simply continues the pattern:

T – W – W – H – W – W – W – H

If you prefer to think in sections:

T → 2 Whole steps → Half step → 3 Whole steps → Half step, or maybe:

T 2W - H - 3W - H.

This formula never changes. Only the starting note changes.

That consistency is your anchor.

White Keys, Black Keys

When you apply the formula, you'll notice something quickly:

- C major uses only white keys

- Every other major scale uses a mix of white and black keys

Example:

F major

F – G – A – B♭ – C – D – E – F

G major

G – A – B – C – D – E – F♯ – G

The black keys are not random. They appear because you follow the formula correctly.

And remember: the musical alphabet must move in order.

D–E–G♭ is incorrect, because G doesn't follow E in the alphabet.

D–E–F♯ is correct because the letters stay in proper sequence.

About Fingerings (For Now)

For this book, you don't need to master every scale in every key. C major is sufficient for understanding the concept, but this fingering also works for the RH in G—D—A—E—B.

Right-hand fingering:

1–2–3_1–2–3–4–5

The underscore represents the thumb passing under the third finger to continue into the upper position. It's helpful to think of the scale as having a lower and an upper pentascale position.

As you approach the thumb crossing:

- Play lightly

- Tuck the thumb

- Release each note cleanly

- Slide the hand to the right

- Allow the thumb to arrive naturally

Avoid twisting the wrist. Think lateral movement, not rotation.

It feels natural to want to help the thumb by turning the hand, but this puts the fingers out of alignment with the keys.

Play slowly. Accuracy first.

- Hear the scale

- See and feel the pattern

- Understand where the half steps and whole steps live

At the piano

- Play one complete major scale slowly

- Say the numbers aloud: 1-2-3-4-5-6-7-1

- Then sing the letter names

Keep finger numbers and scale degrees conceptually separate—but coordinated physically.

Away from the piano

Sing the letter sequence starting on different notes.

Example:

C—D—E—F—G—A—B—C

G—A—B—C—D—E—F#—G

☐ Forward

☐ Backward

The goal is clarity, not speed

Why This Matters

When you return to your chart work, you'll notice something: Melodies often travel beyond the pentascale. Now you have the full scale range available.

Pentascale thinking still informs your chords.

Complete scale thinking expands your melody.

Same system. Broader range.

Chapter 10 (continued)

Behind the Scenes: How Melody Sits on the Chords

This is a behind-the-scenes look at the song. You wouldn't normally write all of this out, but doing it really helps things click at the piano.

In this version, we slow the song down so you can see how the melody lines up with:

- Each chord

- Each syllable or word

When a chord appears, you identify which note of the chord is on top—that's the melody position (such as **C1** or **F5**).

Each new chord has its own numbers starting on 1. When the melody travels outside or between the 1-3-5, such as the 2, 4, or 6, we track how the melody moves up or down from the chord's home tone 1. Keeping this in mind is very helpful to avoid confusion.

Why This Matters

When you understand where the melody sits on the chord, your playing sounds connected, confident, and musical—not random.

Instead of guessing, your hands know where to go, and your ear starts leading the way.

I've worked the first few lines below. Note names are provided to guide you, but you would normally figure this out by ear when listening to a recording. Let the direction of the melody determine whether the next note is higher or lower than the previous note.

5 C1 3 1 3   2 F5   3 C5

A-ma - zi - ng Grace, how sweet the sound

g c   e   c   e   d   c   a   g

5   C1   3-1 3   2 G1

That saved a-a   wretch like me

g   c   e-c e   d   g

Your Turn

Now finish the rest on your own.

_ C_ _ _ _ _   _ F_ _ _ C_

I   on - ce   w - as lost, but now I am found

_   Am_ _ _ G6 _ C_

Was blind, b - ut now I   see

Application

Time to Play Your Arrangement

You're now set up for a simple yet sophisticated sounding solo piano version of Amazing Grace.

You already have:

- Melody
- Chord positions

Now add the bass line like you learned in chapter 6.

As you play your hands together, you'll need to make a few fingering decisions. There isn't always one "correct" choice—but to be a real pianist, you have to choose. It will take a concerted effort, but good fingering—consistently followed—is the surest way to gain proper muscle memory.

Think of fingering as the ballet of the hands. Good fingering allows the music to move smoothly, naturally, and gracefully.

Reminder

Don't rush this.

This is not about speed—it's about control, balance, and sound.

If something feels awkward, stop and fix it.

Good habits form here.

One Phrase at a Time

Work in short phrases, not the whole song.

- Play one lyric phrase slowly

- Listen for how the melody sits on the chord

- Make fingering choices and commit to them

- Repeat until it feels natural

Then connect the phrases together.

That's how an arrangement comes together—one musical thought at a time.

Chapter 10 — Once More with Spice

Here's one more version of Amazing Grace. This chart adds a little spice:

- More movement in the bass line using slash chords

- A suspended 4

Slash Chords

A slash chord uses two letters separated by a forward slash.

Example:

C/E

- The letter on the left is the chord

- The letter on the right is the bass note

C/E means:

- Play a **C** chord in your right hand

- Play **E** in the bass

Why this matters:

Slash chords allow the bass line to walk instead of jump, adding motion and interest without clutter.

Continue using melody positions: Examples: **C1/E—C3/E—C5/E.**

Suspensions

A suspended 4 (sus4) is when you temporarily replace the 3 of a chord with the 4.

This creates a gentle tension—as if the harmony is hanging in the air. Play 1-4-5 before resolving (returning and releasing tension) back to 1-3-5.

Suspensions are often used on the final home chord, just before the ending, giving the listener a moment to lean in... and breathe. Subtle—but powerful.

For the final chart, begin by identifying the melody position chords and the melody notes that correspond to each syllable of the lyrics.

To create a solo piano arrangement, add a bass line beneath the chords. When accompanying a worship band, you may simply comp the chords—playing them with a straightforward rhythm. Steady, even quarter notes work well. They maintain the pulse while providing warm, supportive harmony.

When comping, you may include the bass line or leave it out. Try both ways. Amazing Grace is in 3/4 time, so each measure contains three beats.

Final Chart for WORSHIP MUSIC HOW TO: PIANO — BOOK 1

Amazing Grace

```
  C           F          C
Amazing Grace, how sweet the sound


    C               G
That saved a wretch like me


  C      C/E    F       C
I once was lost, but now I am found


G/B Am        C/G G/B   Csus4   C
Was  blind, but now   I        see
```

I've intentionally left this version sparse in terms of extra guidance. By now, you should be able to handle it on your own. But here's a few hints: the LH must travel outside the pentascale, and the **Csus4** at the end will be an inversion. Have fun!

Chapter 11

The Last Will Be First

Prepare to Worship

Last things first.

Jesus said, "So those who are last now will be first then, and those who are first will be last."

Matthew 20:16, NLT

I'm not going to preach a sermon on this passage. I just want to use the principle behind it to talk about the order of things as we prepare to worship. Although this is the final chapter of the book, it is first in importance.

Before anything else—before you practice, rehearse, or sit down at the piano for a worship service—pray. It seems simple. And it is essential.

Jesus said, "Seek the Kingdom of God above all else, and live righteously, and he will give you everything you need."

Matthew 6:33, NLT

If you want to be a worship musician, this is where you begin—with your spiritual attitude and your personal growth.

Yes, we must learn to play our instruments with excellence. That matters. It's part of "everything you need." But even more important is our character, and whether it reflects the character of Christ.

It's easy for pride to sneak in when we play in front of people—whether the congregation is large or small. So we pray.

As Jesus also said, "Pray that you will not give in to temptation."

Luke 22:40, NLT

A Simple Guideline for Preparation

This is not complicated.

It's about order, not perfection.

Pray

- Pray for focus and clarity

- Pray before you practice

- Pray before rehearsal

- Pray before you play

You are a lead worshiper, whether you're at the piano, the keyboard, or somewhere in the background. Be one in the truest sense—honoring God not only with your playing, but with your life. Let that reality shape your worship.

Listen

Listen for the guidance of the Holy Spirit.

Jesus said, "But when the Father sends the Advocate as my representative—that is, the Holy Spirit—he will teach you everything and will remind you of everything I have told you." John 14:26, NLT

- Ask the Holy Spirit to teach you

- Listen to the recordings of the songs on your worship list

- Have the chart in front of you while you listen

- Pay attention to:

  - the song form

  - where sections repeat or change

  - moments that feel exposed or delicate

Make notes if something stands out—anything that might help you later.

Sing the lyrics. Know what is being said. You are helping set the table for the Word of God to be presented. Understanding the message matters.

Schedule

Carve out time in your day to pray and to practice.

As you move through your day, you know you need to practice. But if you don't schedule that time, evening arrives quickly. You're tired. The day is gone. And the piano never happened.

Chances are, you'll procrastinate.

Take it from me—one who knows.

Consistency beats intensity every time.

 PREPARATION CHECK

(Optional, but powerful)

Before a worship service, ask yourself:

☐ Have I prayed—not just played?

☐ Have I listened to the songs carefully?

☐ Do I have a clear understanding of the song form?

☐ Do I know where the breaks and rhythmic accents are?

☐ Do I understand the message of the lyrics?

☐ Have I prepared faithfully, not frantically?

If the answer is yes, you're ready.

Appendix

The examples in this appendix are sparse. This is intentional. The goal is more to think in numbers and less in notes on a staff. It's the way we approach Worship charts.

Example 1

Circle of Fifths—Primary Pathway

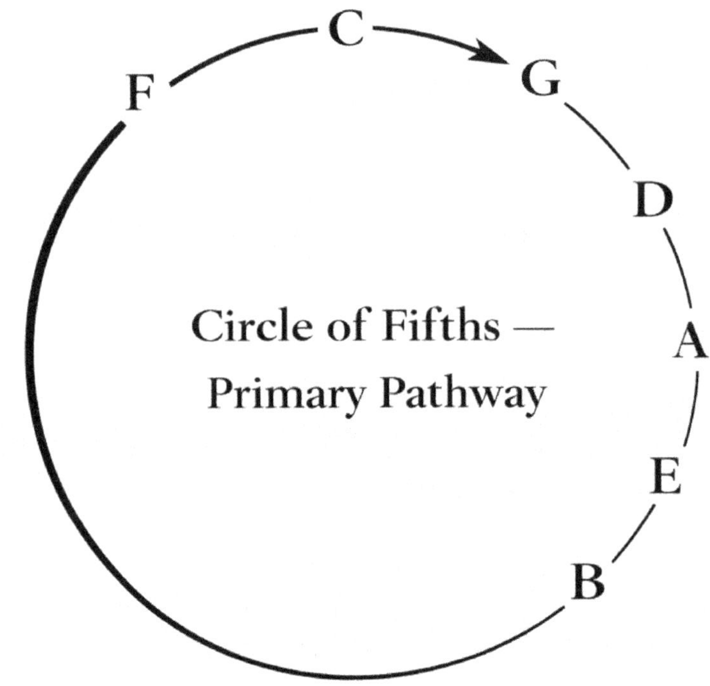

Clockwise: F–C–G–D–A–E–B

Counterclockwise: B–E–A–D–G–C–F

Circle of Fifths — Same Order — Different Pathway

Linear Order - From Lowest to Highest

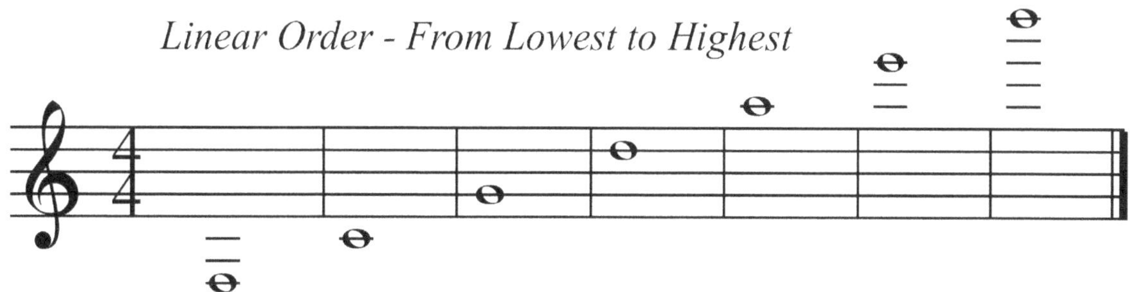

Zigzag Order - Up and Down

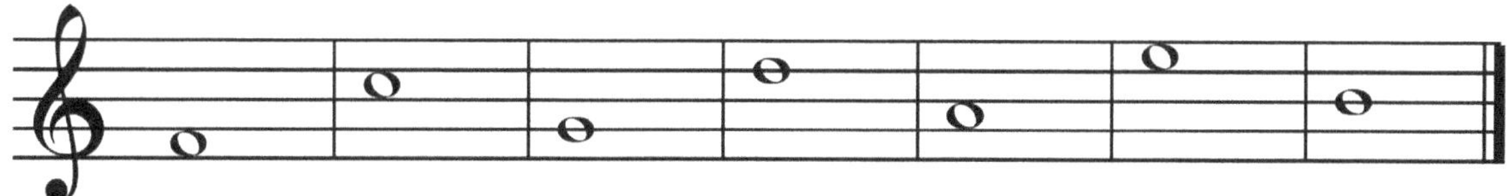

Improvised Order - You Chose

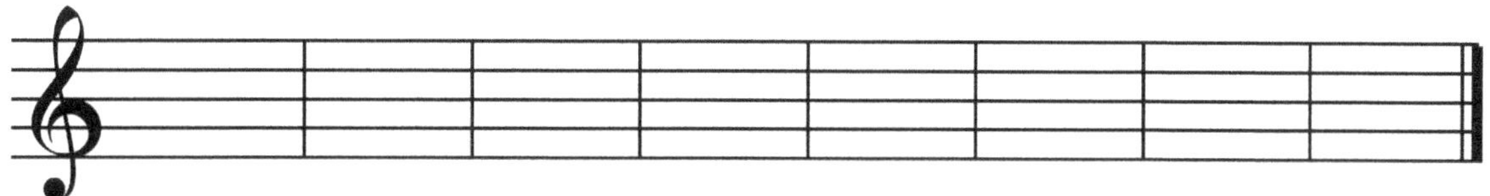

Example 3

Major Pentascale Formula

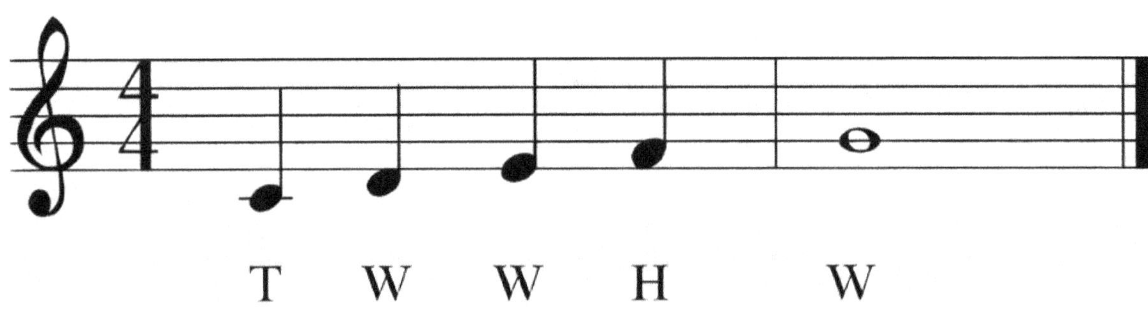

Example 4: Melody Position Triad Inversions

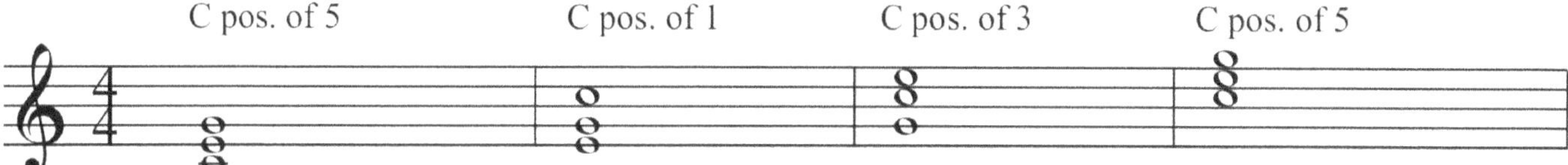

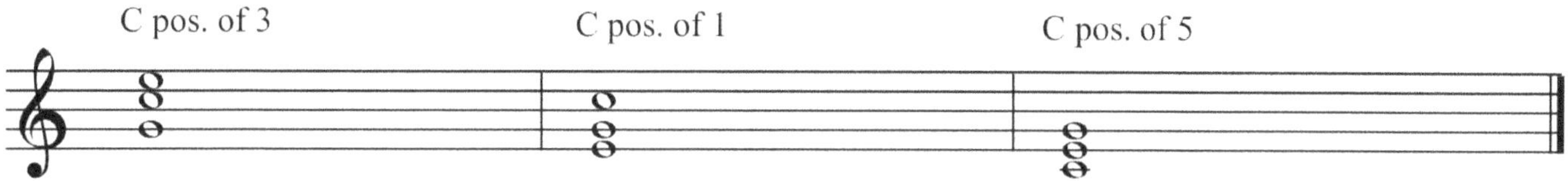

What You Will Be Able To Do

By the time you complete this book and work through the exercises at the piano, you will be able to:

Clearly understand how melody and harmony function in real songs.

Use the Circle of 5ths as a practical pathway for organizing your practice.

Build and play the major pentascales beginning on F-C-G-D-A-E-B.

Hear and feel tonic (1) and dominant (5) relationships.

Play major and minor triad chords with confidence.

Recognize and play melody position chords.

Add simple, supportive bass lines.

Follow and interpret chord charts with growing confidence.

Connect melody, chords, and bass into a clear, usable piano arrangement.

Practice in a way that builds accuracy, control, and musical confidence.

More importantly, you will begin thinking like a real worship pianist—listening carefully, supporting the song, and playing with clarity, intention, and purpose.

Acknowledgments

First, thank you to God—for the gift of music.

To my heart—my wife, Sandra—for your great patience, your greater faith, and your constant love.

Thank you to every student of mine—I learn as much from you as you do from me.

Dr. Gary Smart—for allowing me the freedom to create.

William Alexander—for guiding me in the discipline to create, and for leading me to Christ.

Final Thoughts

I sincerely hope that this book—WORSHIP MUSIC HOW TO: PIANO — BOOK 1—has been worth your time, effort, and investment.

If you'd like to share your experiences, feel free to reach out. Your insights may help shape the direction of future editions.

Thank you for taking the journey—and for serving faithfully.

Todd G. Kelly

soundmindtgk@yahoo.com

About the Author

Todd G. Kelly is a teacher, composer, pianist, and producer with more than three decades of experience helping musicians grow in skill and confidence at the piano.

Worship Music How To: Piano — Book 1 reflects his belief that music theory should be simple, useful, and immediately applicable at the keyboard.

Through his teaching studio, Piano Plus, Todd has worked with students of all ages and levels, focusing on practical musicianship, creativity, and the joy of making music. His approach combines clear theory, real-world playing skills, and encouragement designed to help students become confident, expressive pianists.

Todd plays piano and keyboards for worship at Sagebrush Church and teaches at the Sagebrush Music Academy at the Riverside Campus in Albuquerque, New Mexico.

His music is represented by major production libraries including BMG Production Music and Warner Chappell Production Music—with credits appearing on international broadcasts and media, including ION, Univision, BBC and the Hong Kong International Film Festival.